Flirting With Spirituality
Live your purpose! Spread joy! Connect with the magic!

by Jill Spiegel
with Joe Brozic

ISBN 09643325-2-3

Published by Joe Brozic
              Goal Getters

Write to: Goal Getters
              3943 Chowen Ave. S
              Minneapolis, MN 55410

Phone:    612-925-5814
Fax:       612-922-8241
Website: Flirtnow.com

Printed in the United States Of America
Written - Jill Spiegel
Edited and Published - Joe Brozic
Cover Design - Jill Spiegel and Joe Brozic
Proofread - Laura Jervis
Production- Gail Furseth and Jay Witta

Jill Spiegel, spiritual motivator and author of "Flirting For Success" and "The Pocket Pep Talk," owns Goal Getters with her business partner and husband Joe Brozic.

Order "Flirting With Spirituality" from
Goal Getters
3943 Chowen Ave. S.
Minneapolis, MN 55410

Phone:    612-925-5814
Fax:       612-922-8241
website: Flirtnow.com

# Table Of Contents

I was watching the Oprah show one afternoon and her guest was Director Steven Spielberg. I watched and listened intently for awhile. Then I drifted off....

.....Hmmmm...Steven Spielberg...... He seems like such a good person.....Spie-lberg...Spie-gel.....Hmmm....maybe one day our paths will cross......

One week later, I went to New York City to visit my grandmother for Thanksgiving. I walked out of a boutique on Madison Avenue and there he was standing right on the corner–Steven Spielberg! To some that's called coincidence. I call it spiritual magic, and I've been flirting with spirituality as long as I can remember.

When I was a little girl, my friends and I had a toy we loved called The Magic 8 Ball. It was an oversized black pool ball with an 8 painted on it. It also had a little window that flashed brief messages such as, "It is so," or "Not likely," or "Ask again later." We would shake the 8 ball and ask question after question: "Will I get an A on my quiz? It is so!" "Does Peter like me? It says yes!"

One of the best parts of our exciting ritual was we understood that while the 8 ball was magical, we also knew to trust our own magic. So if an answer appeared that didn't fit our wish or instinct, we always had a solution, "Shake it up and ask it again!" That's exactly how flirting with spirituality works. It's about reading the magic that's all around us, and then listening to our magic within.

Spirituality is our own creative process, which makes each of us a spiritual artist. In my workshops on the subject, I have met hundreds of people, like you and me, who have shared their way of flirting with spirituality.

Penny told our class, "When I'm reading a book and my mind starts to wander with this problem or that one, I use my book as a source for answers. I close my eyes and my book. Then I ask a question and with my eyes still closed I open the book to any page. I point to a spot on the page and open my eyes. The word or sentence I land on always seems to have a clue for me."

Aaron then added, "I find magic in my horoscope, which I love to read every morning. There have been times that my horoscope had such a clear message which spoke to me, that I'd cut it out and tape it in my planner. I remember once I had to give a speech in front of a committee, and I was so nervous. Then I read my morning horoscope which said, 'Your words have the power of authority. Think like a leader.' That was just the pep talk I needed."

Ken also shared his artistic style, "I was driving with my wife and she was telling me something really important, but I wasn't paying attention. I started worrying about work, which I knew was the wrong choice in the moment. She needed me. Then I noticed a passing billboard which read, "Are you Listening?" I really felt like something above was speaking to me. I stopped thinking about work and listened to my wife."

You are a spiritual artist too. This book is a guide to help you express your spirituality, celebrate your creative power and unleash your magic.

Imagine you wake up one morning and discover that you are magic! Before, your whole world was in black and white. Now it's in full color! You discover that you have the amazing ability to find a secret gift in every event, every encounter, every moment. You thrive in this magical adventure and you spread joy wherever you go.

Well, guess what?

YOU REALLY ARE MAGIC!

Want to be sure? Then, take The Magic Quiz. Has one or more of these things ever happened to you? (If yes, go ahead and jot down what happened.)

1. Have you ever been thinking about somebody and then ran into them soon after?

2. Have you ever had a coincidence that felt like more than pure chance?

3. Has a solution to a problem suddenly popped in your head to give you instant clarity?

4. Have you ever felt a presence protecting or watching you?

5. Have you ever had a dream and find that elements of it come true later?

6.  Have you ever felt a strong inner voice urging you one way or another?

7.  Have you ever had a sixth sense about someone immediately?

8.  Have you ever been thinking about a song, then turn the radio on and it's playing?

9.  Have you ever felt "called" or inspired towards an activity, hobby or job?

10. Have you ever "known" the outcome of something before it happened?

11. Have you ever had a little or big wish come true?

You proved that you have spiritual magic – a magnificent transparent thread that weaves inside of you and connects with everything and everyone around you through a wondrous tapestry. The more you tap into this magic, the sooner everything you want and desire will flow right to you!

This book is your guide for magnifying your special powers. We will explore five fun and simple ways to flirt with spirituality. It's just a start, but it works immediately. Once you get the idea, then you take over. You keep on flirting with spirituality your way, in your own style,

which is always the best way.

I've always felt that life was magical. When I was a little girl, I loved to study a rock or stare at a cloud. To my delight and wonder, I'd discover a face emerging, a face smiling at me! I had a deep sense that everything around me was alive, and somehow all connected.

I also sensed that something loving (and invisible) was protecting me. When I was about six, I had a mysterious incident at summer day camp. I didn't know how to swim, and when no one was watching me, I foolishly hopped in the gigantic pool and found myself under water at the deep end. Gasping and paddling, the word "help!" flashed in my mind. And then out of nowhere, I saw two big hands reach for me and lift me out of the water!

Whoosh! I was pulled way up ...ahhh air! I looked at my rescuer. He was an old man with a kind face and white hair. Who was he? I had never seen him before. He smiled warmly and said, "You don't belong here," and he took me back to the edge of the shallow side. He gently placed me down and when I looked up to see him, he had vanished! Was he an angel?

Has anyone ever suddenly appeared to help you?

Many years later, I was walking through a mall when I saw a little girl crying. I asked her where her mommy was and she didn't know. I took her hand and we walked from store to store looking for her mother. As we were scanning our ninth store, the little girl shouted "Mommy!"' A woman ran towards her and they hugged and cried and giggled for awhile. I was going to talk to the woman, but she didn't notice me and she seemed so happy. So I waved to the little girl and left. A few months later I was in that store again. The clerk said to me, "That woman whose child you found was looking for you, but she said you vanished."Was I an angel? Perhaps we all are.

Have you ever appeared at the right time to help someone?

As I grew, I began to feel that the magic wasn't just around me, it also lived inside of me and everyone else. In a journal, I recorded every wish I had that came true. I started to ask my friends if they ever felt this magical connection, and I discovered I had plenty of company! More and more I came to realize that life was rooting for all of us and that there was a deeper meaning to everything.

Each and everyone has our own special way of connecting with the world spiritually. We have our own truth and path, and the answers are within ourselves, and all around us. All we have to do is learn to tap into our special power.

Flirting with spirituality is creating joy in yourself and others by connecting with the magical side of life.

Five fun and instant ways to unleash your magic are:

M – MEANING
You are the artist of your own destiny.
Follow your heart.

A – AWARENESS
Life gives you magical clues to help you find joy.
Pay attention.

G – GRATITUDE
Everything happens for a reason.
Give thanks and feel instant energy.

I – IMAGINE
Thoughts are real.
Imagine the best for yourself and others.

C – CONNECT
Magic is everywhere.
Reach out, Life joyfully reaches back.

And of course any other way you think of! Let's look at them one at a time...

**Meaning:**
**You are the artist of your own destiny.**


**Follow your heart.**

Imagine you are a painter. You are standing in front of a canvas with your paint brush and palette of colors. You choose certain colors and paint them in various shapes and expressions. Then you stand back for a few moments and see how your picture looks and feels so far.

You really are that painter and that picture is your life. We all come to life with a blank canvas. The choices we make are like painting new colors, creating and adding to our current life picture. At any time we can pick new colors or paint new shapes. As artists, we are in constant creation of our destiny!

That's what you're doing this very second. You are making a choice. You are choosing joy.

And you deserve it!

We all have magical gifts and desires which lead us to our life's purpose.

We can express this purpose in every moment, through:
interacting,
working,
volunteering,
being,
mentoring,
thinking,
leading,
creating,
connecting,
and countless other ways.

Living on purpose gives us meaning and joy, and in turn we give joy to others.

In this chapter, we'll explore some ways to express our purpose and bring meaning and joy to every situation:

## "What can I offer?" Brings Instant Purpose

Has anyone ever stopped you for directions? Didn't it make you feel great to help them out? It's amazing how a little bit of giving or sharing can bring so much satisfaction and meaning. We can always find instant purpose and spread joy in every situation just by asking one question: how can I help? By offering our best selves, we increase our magic and change the lives around us.

Phyllis told our class, "I work in a small office. There was a lot of negative inside gossip. I decided to make my secret purpose to stop the gossip by not participating and setting an example. Little by little, my co-workers started to change, one person at a time. Now our work environment is much more open, healthy and supportive, and I feel great."

Harvey shared with us, "My prime purpose is to be a great dad. I didn't have a father growing up, and I really missed that. When my son was born, I knew that I could be the dad I had always wished for. My child gives my life meaning."

Wanda told our class: "One thing I do is over tip and surprise people. Whenever I take a taxi or am waited on in a restaurant, I give a tip beyond 20%. People are always so grateful, happy and surprised. One cab driver was having a terrible day and when I said 'Keep the change', he beamed and said, 'That made my day.'"

Drake found that defining his purpose helped him feel more comfortable in social situations, "I used to judge myself every time I went to a party or function. I'd get so nervous thinking 'What are they going to think of me?' I'd work myself into a panic judging myself through other people's eyes. Then I learned that I was asking myself the wrong question. Instead of 'What are they going to think of me?' I could be asking myself 'What can I offer them?' That question gave me purpose and power, melting away the fear. Now I had something to give to people; a smile, being a good listener, my warmth. I stopped judging myself and focused on giving. I enjoy life so much more now."

Say the magic words, **"What can I offer?"**

Presto! Instant purpose

## Our Life Painting Is Always Evolving

Another way we find meaning and purpose is through our jobs or careers, which change and evolve throughout our lives. As we grow, we learn that every experience prepares us for another. We are destiny artists. We have the power to create our next direction.

Before I started my own motivational business, I was a recruiting and training manager for a sales company. For the first several years I found this job challenging and thrilling. I came aboard after college graduation when I started as a salesperson, (selling knives and cutlery in people's homes,) and then I moved into management, (recruiting and teaching others how to build rapport and sell.) Through this job, I was able to motivate groups and individuals and sharpen my speaking skills. I soon discovered I had a message that could help create happiness and success for everyone. I longed to inspire more and more people.

It was time for a change. I sat down with myself and did some personal investigating. What is my purpose and how can I shape my life to express it?

Here was my list:

| | |
|---|---|
| What do I love to do the most? | I love to inspire, entertain and talk. |
| What am I best at? | Connecting with people, motivating, being in front of groups. |
| What's important to me? | Inspiring people, recognition, freedom, creative expression. |
| How can I help others? | By teaching them how to follow their hearts and connect with others. To lead by example. |

## Bringing Purpose To Work

The key to our purpose lies in our hearts, the deepest part of our magic. If we want to change our work picture, which is an expression of our purpose, all we need to do is go within and ask ourselves certain questions. Here are some sample lists from past course participants:

| | |
|---|---|
| What do I love to do the most? | I love to play golf. |
| What am I best at? | Organizing and managing. |
| What do I want? | I want to play golf and have a job that gives me some freedom and little pressure. |
| How can I help others? | By helping them relieve their stress. |

Fay left her stressful job and became the full-time manager at a golf course where she lives and works, and thrives.

Here's another:

| | |
|---|---|
| What do I love to do the most? | I love to make art and I love cars. |
| What am I best at? | Drawing and connecting with people one to one. |
| What do I want? | Personal fulfillment and the ability to support my family. |
| How can I help others? | By helping them make smart safe choices and being a loving parent and husband. |

Greg was successful in the graphic arts field full time, but he yearned to be around cars. He decided to follow his heart and sell cars full time, and turn his art career into a free lance side business. This shift brought him new fulfillment and focus.

Now it's your turn!

What do I love to do the most?

What am I best at?

What's important to me?

How can I help others?

I see a theme emerging:

## Our Purpose Is Tied To Our Story

If your life was a movie, what would be the theme, the lesson? When we stand back from our lives, and look at the big picture there is an underlying theme, a story...a clue.

One of my course participants came to class to discover her purpose. Debbie said she always felt she was meant to entertain, but when she tried acting and stand-up comedy, she felt empty. "I just don't know what I'm supposed to do, but I love making people laugh."

"What's your life story?" I asked her. Now in her forties, she said "My story is about a woman, me, who became a single mother at a very young age and how that made her life extremely challenging. My movie has been quite a drama and now I'm ready to turn it into a comedy!" After she told me that, her face suddenly lit up. "Hey! maybe that's my purpose!"

There was her answer. She joined up with her daughter, who loves to write, and together they started a newsletter for single mothers and their families. "I love it! While our message is informative, we lighten the tone with humor. We get to help others laugh and handle their lives. I've found so much meaning. And being with my daughter is amazing for both of us."

Take a look at your own movie. You are the lead character.
Ask yourself:

What has been my story?

Has it been a comedy, drama, thriller, action, all of those or something else?

What are the major lessons?

How can my story and lessons help others?

Where do I want to go next?

How can I make that happen?

You're not only the star, you write the script!

## Purpose Comes From Within

As artists of our destiny, we can change our future any time and create a new life picture. Yolanda, from my course, shared her story:

"I had a glamorous corporate job in advertising. I made a lot of money and met a lot of famous people. I always had thought this 'dream job' would make be happy. 'Isn't this success?' I'd say to myself. But I was miserable.

The worse I felt, the more I bought. But, none of my new things not the clothes, the car, the jewelry, none of it cheered me up. In fact, the more I acquired, the more responsibility I had, the worse I felt inside. I tried to keep busy and ignore my emptiness, until the day I was about to be promoted. That's when I knew. Is this what I want for the next several years... more misery?

I asked myself, if I could do anything in the world, what would I do? I've always been excellent with color and design, and I used to draw all the time. Deep down inside, I guess I've always wanted to be an artist, and I want to help children in some way. At that point I re-shaped my life and took a new direction.

I quit that job, sold my things, moved into a small house, and turned the den into my art studio. Simplifying was so liberating! I started sharing my art with underprivileged children by holding free art classes at community centers. I scaled down my 'things' and nurtured my spirit. Everything has fallen into place and I've never been happier."

## Keep Track Of The Magic

The magical thing about following your heart is that the universe will immediately assist you. Pursue your passion with patience and integrity and everything you need will appear.

Keep a journal of coincidences and synchronicities that happen to you along the way. Make a note every time a wish comes true or something miraculously falls into place. You will see that magic is working. Here are some snippets from journals of other destiny artists.

Rena, who decided to start her own practice shared: "I had no idea where to find space for my yoga therapy practice. Then I ran into an old neighbor while shopping and she told me she was leasing space at her massage studio. It was perfect!"

I wrote this is my journal when I landed my first print piece:
"The reporter goofed the title of my class in his article. But a publisher loved the title he read about and called me to write a book!"

Sam was discouraged until......
"Nobody was buying my art, and I was just about to give up. I started to look for a job in the paper when the phone rang. Three of my pictures had just sold! I knew it was a sign to stick with it."

I've seen this magic happen for hundreds of people including myself. When we follow our spirit, we find miracles. Have you ever had that feeling that things were miraculously falling into place? What happened?

## Purpose Blossoms With Self-Definition

When we define ourselves by externals, we constantly need approval from others, which ironically means we're powerless. When we define ourselves by internals, our magic is dependent on no one but ourselves, and we instantly become all powerful and joyful.

| | |
|---|---|
| Externals = ego | Internals = selfhood |
| I am my occupation. | I am creative. |
| I am my possessions. | I am my spirit. |
| I am what others think. | I am what I think. |
| I am my appearance. | I am my soul. |
| I am better than them. | I am equally magical. |
| I am an image. | I am me. |

Ego = externals = false self = illusion = insecurity
Selfhood = internals = authentic self = truth = security

How would your answer this question?
**"What am I about?"**

## Meaning is in Leading

A wise young woman, who was a college sophomore at the time, once called me for some mentoring and career advice. When we met, we ended up teaching each other.

She told me that two of her professors were each urging her to run for president of a different committee. "I don't know what to do. They each say I should do this....," she explained. I looked her in the eyes and said, "Has anybody asked you what you want?"

She was quiet for moment and said, "Well no." "What do you want?" I asked her and she said, "I want neither committee. I want to be president of the journalism club." "Then I think you should be president of journalism club," I echoed.

"Thank you." She smiled. That was all she needed to hear.

At the time, I was consumed with goals and had been putting a lot of pressure on myself. My next question reflected my state of mind and also gave her added subtle pressure, "What do you want to do when you graduate in two years?" That's when she mentored me. With strength and dignity she said, "I believe that right now the best thing for me to do is explore my interests. I'm not worried about what happens in two years. I'm taking it one day at a time."

"Thank you." I smiled. That was just what I needed to learn.
We are all leaders to each other.

We can lead in every moment.

Who has been a leader to you or inspired you?

In what ways can you lead or inspire others?

To know what you believe,
to define yourself, to live with honesty,
integrity and
strength.
Success is inner peace.

## Meaning Leads To Abundance

When you follow your heart, you'll always find what you need. Bertice, who took my class, explained, "I decided I wanted to be a massage therapist and switch my career direction. I knew there were many therapists like me who had practices in this city, but there's always room for more. I earned my license, went forward with confidence, and I had no trouble finding clients." We need never worry or fear. There is an endless supply of magic for all of us. Choose to live in abundance.

| Scarcity thinking: | VS. | Abundance Thinking: |
|---|---|---|
| The universe is limited. | | In the universe, all is possible. |
| If someone else succeeds, I can't. | | We all can succeed at the same time. |
| I must compete to win. | | Helping others helps myself. |
| I can't have it all. | | I can have what I desire, and I deserve it. |
| I have to grab this small window of opportunity. | | Everything happens at the perfect time. |
| Life has to be rough. | | We are here to experience joy. |

Scarcity = Fear = Illusion
Abundance = Love = Truth = YOU!

# Fear Is Imagined

I remember when I decided to try selling knives, most people thought I was crazy. Without seeing the product or my sales presentation, they'd jump to conclusions and say, "That sounds awful!" I wondered if I was the only one who encountered such discouragement until I arrived for my first day of training.

My manager asked the group, "Did anyone have a negative response from their friends or family?" I raised my hand and looked around the room. All hands were raised. He advised us, "Stay positive and believe in yourself. All the negativity you encountered came from people who are imagining the worst. Just wait until they see those knives! Remember, fear really is false expectations appearing real." That's true! I thought. They had never seen the knives. They were just imagining. I felt much better.

When you hear fear come from yourself or anyone else, calm the fear down. Talk to it, tell it the truth.

| When you panic or fear: | Answer yourself with: |
|---|---|
| What if I fail? | The universe is on my side, I cannot fail. |
| I have to hurry! | I have no time limits. Everything happens at the right time. |
| I must chase it! | I can let go and source it towards me. |

| When someone tells you: | You can lead and help them: |
|---|---|
| "Can you make money at that?" | "I believe when you do what you love, the money follows." |
| "Isn't that a crowded field?" | "There's always room for more." |
| "That's going to be hard." | "Yes, it's rewarding and fun. It doesn't feel like work." |

Fearful people are actually in pain because they have forgotten they are magical, but you haven't.

You are a leader.

You melt the fear away.

## Recipes For Instant Purpose

Spread joy wherever you go and you will create instant purpose. The following list is a way to inspire others and bring joy to every situation:

- smile and look people in the eyes
- pay a sincere compliment
- open a door for someone else
- giggle
- think positively about everyone you meet
- stay calm
- encourage someone
- look for the lesson in every situation
- be "in the moment"
- let someone else go first
- give up needing to be right
- help someone less fortunate than you
- define yourself from within
- start a conversation
- be grateful
- be kind to everyone
- be kind to yourself

What are some other ways to bring instant purpose?

Let's take a quick review of Meaning:

    * You are the artist of your destiny.
    * Ask the magic words, "What can I offer?"
    * Following your heart brings purpose and happiness.
    * Creating your own path increases your magic.
    * Internal self-definition is true power.
    * Meaning is in leading. We are leaders to each other.
    * Scarcity is an illusion, abundance is truth.
    * All fear is imagined, love is real.
    * Practice instant purpose.

Bring Meaning to
                 every situation
                 every person

                 every moment

**Awareness:**
**Life gives you magical clues to help you find joy.**

**Pay attention.**

Imagine you are a spirit and you came to earth with one mission, to find joy. To assist you in this mission, the universe provides you with magical mystical clues. Some of these clues are tangible, some are invisible.

You really are that spirit and the universe is providing you with clues every day. All you have to do is pay attention and joy is yours.

# Life Is A Magical Treasure Hunt

Clues to our joy are all around us. When our hearts desire something, the universe responds by giving us a variety of hints on how to get there. Discovering those clues and interpreting them is what makes our journey so meaningful and so much fun!

There are many clues and ways in which life communicates with us. There are:

1. Intuition or Feeling Clues

2. Sign Clues

3. Innervoice Clues

4. Coincidence Clues

5. Guiding Spirit Clues

6. Event and Encounter Clues

and

7. Any other kind that work for you!

## #1. Intuition or Feeling Clues

I remember when I landed the knife salesperson job, my mom cried, "I can't believe my daughter is going into strange people's home with knives!" "Don't worry Ma," I tried to calm her, "I'm the one holding the knives!" She wasn't the only one who protested. My dad had the company investigated and most of my friends also questioned my judgement. I could understand their concerns.

But, I couldn't ignore my feelings. With all the warnings and obvious reservations, I just had a strong feeling I should try this job. My gut feeling was right. I found joy in developing my skills, connecting with customers and encouraging my office teammates. Still, even more magic was in store.

One day my manager called me in his office. He told me I was doing so well that he wanted me to become a branch manager and open up a new territory- in Minneapolis! I couldn't believe it. You see, deep down inside I hadn't always wanted to be knife a salesperson, I've wanted to be Mary Tyler Moore! When I was little, I'd watch The Mary Tyler Moore Show from my suburban Chicago home and wish that someday I'd be Mary, independent and living in Minneapolis. My feelings were right. Despite all the warnings, my intuition knew my knives would bring me fulfillment and lead me to Mary!

Our feelings and intuition are magic expressions of our spirit. They link us to who we are, what we need, and how we want to continue to create ourselves. Our best decisions are made when we listen to our feelings and our intuition.

Trevor's intuition protected him, "I went for an interview at a small company that seemed reputable. I was excited on the way there, but when I arrived, I had the worst feeling in my stomach. It wasn't nerves, more like a feeling something wasn't right. I didn't take the job and it was a good thing. The company closed down the following week."

Henrietta told us, "I let out my dog in the fenced in backyard every morning for five years. Never a problem. One morning I let him outside, but minutes later I had a strange feeling something was wrong. When I walked back out, I noticed that someone had opened our side gate door and the dog was gone! I was so scared! Luckily he didn't run very far. He was in the front yard waiting for me. Dogs must have intuition too."

Caren shared with the class, "I needed an assistant at work. After interviewing several candidates, I decided to choose this one gal who may have not been the obvious choice. She had very little experience, but instantly she gave me such a warm feeling. I felt I could trust her and my intuition was right. She's been invaluable."

When has your intuition guided you?


How do you recognize it?


What is it telling you about yourself and your life right now?

To get in touch with your intuition:
- Pay attention to all your feelings, never ignore them.
- Notice your physical responses to situations, people and ideas. Do you have a sinking stomach, warm tingles, a sense of lightness? All feelings are clues.
- Express your feelings openly and honestly.
- Spend some quiet, or silent, time alone.

## #2. Sign Clues

My grandmother had recently passed away and left me a little pill box that says, "When this you see, remember me." One night I went to give a speech and in the audience was an older woman, seated alone, who looked and acted so much like my grandmother! She came up to me after my speech and said, "I think you are very talented. Be patient. All things happen at the right time." Her voice sounded like my grandmother's and those words were just what I needed to hear. I felt the chills.

The next morning I asked for a sign that my grandmother was watching over me. My husband and I took our dog, Buddy, for a walk around the lake. Buddy stopped to scratch and Joe said "Jill Look!" There laying on the ground was a rock with the word "remember" perfectly carved in it. I instantly thought of Grandmother's pill box, "remember me" and the mysterious woman who reminded me of her. It was my sign!"

A sign can be a feeling, a coincidence, an encounter, a dream, an object, a comment, a guiding spirit, anything that speaks to us or seems to be sending us a message. Signs come to us constantly when we need them, especially when we pay attention and when we ask.

Bill, an aspiring teacher, shared his sign, "I was an accountant for five years, but all along I really wanted to teach grade school. I had been wrestling with this life change for some time and then I found my clue. I was waiting in line for my dry cleaning, when I heard, 'Is that you Billy?' I turned around and there was my wonderful fourth grade teacher, Mrs. Bloom! It had been so many years! Even before we started chatting, I knew I had my answer."

Elizabeth felt her answer came in a dream, "I went on a date with a guy I liked, but I had some reservations. He seemed quite distant, and I was feeling both excited and confused about him. Should I go out with him again or should I protect myself? When I went to sleep that night, he was in my dream! We were on a roller coaster ride and it just kept going and going. I woke up feeling exhausted, but also very clear. I knew it was a sign."

A clue is anything that works for you.
You are the artist.
You pick the clues that speak to you.

When have you felt you saw a sign? What happened?

How often do you think about signs?

To increase the appearance of signs in your life you can:
- Be open to receiving them at all times.
- Ask for them whenever you need one.
- Pay attention to subtle clues.
- Record your signs in a journal.

## #3. Innervoice Clues

During a major turning point in my life, my innervoice whispered to me with such simple and powerful wisdom, I knew I had to listen. I was away on a trip taking a mountain hike. As I walked up the mountain, absorbing the beauty around me, my innervoice suddenly told me, "Go back to Minneapolis and follow your dream. It's time." Was that my thought? I wondered. It came from my mind, yet it felt like it was someone or something else giving me this important direction. And I knew it was right. I went back to Minneapolis, left my sales job and started my own company. The voice was right. It was time.

Our innervoice lives in our spirit. It is that calm, sure voice deep down inside of us. It whispers to offer us wisdom.

Isabelle told the class, "I had a wonderful, but strange innervoice communication. I was waiting in line for some fast food and the gal in front of me turned around and smiled. In my mind I heard, 'Talk now,' almost like an instruction. So I struck up a conversation, 'Are you late for work too?' This started a whole conversation about our jobs, which lead to a connection of interests and the next thing you know we ended up opening a business together a year later!"

Your innervoice also may peacefully whisper to you during times of fear or frustration to help you calm down and bring you clarity.

In one of my spirituality seminars, Carl explained, "I was driving down an icy highway and my car started spinning in circles. I couldn't control it, but I was surprised at how calm I felt. And I kept hearing in my mind, 'You are safe.' It turned out I was. The car came to a stop and nothing was hit."

Loraine told us,
"One time a friend made a confusing remark to me that really offended me. The more I thought about her comment, the more upset I became. As I marched around my house feeling my anger build, a sudden whisper brought me instant ease. 'She meant........' the voice explained. This gentle whisper calmed me immediately and helped me understand the comment in a whole new light."

Carmen said, "I was about to scream at my sister, then I heard the word 'breathe.' I followed direction and spared us from a yelling match. My innervoice was right to help me calm down."

When has your innervoice given you a clear message?

What did it say?

How does your innervoice make you feel?

To hear your innervoice more often:
- Take a few minutes every day in silence.
- Write down what your innervoice tells you.
- Stay calm in all situations.
- Ask your innervoice, "What would wisdom say now?"

## #4. Coincidence Clues

I was sitting at a restaurant having breakfast with my sister. She ordered orange juice and I ordered tomato juice. After our drinks had arrived and we had a few sips, I thought to myself, "I'm really craving orange juice more than tomato. I wish I had ordered orange instead." Poof! At that exact moment, the waitress arrived with a glass of orange juice in her hand. "You already brought mine," my sister smiled. "Well," the waitress grinned as she put the drink in front of me, "Then you can have this one for free." What a tiny, but miraculous coincidence! And they happen to all of us, all the time. Coincidences could also be called, spiritual magic in motion. They prove that our thoughts and desires are woven with the universal magic. Coincidences whisper to us: "The magic is with you."

Jamie told our class, "I was supposed to meet my friends at a concert. We picked a meeting spot, but I couldn't find them. I walked around for half an hour and still no luck. So I decided to let go and just enjoy the concert on my own. I found a place on the open lawn. And as soon as I sat down, I felt a tap on the shoulder. It was my friends. I had landed right in front of them and didn't even know it."

Betty explained, "I was away with a tour group in Europe. Although I was having a great time, I was real homesick and missed my family. I was on a train heading for the next city, when who steps on? My cousin! I had heard she was going away this summer, but I didn't know where! We both couldn't believe it! What are the chances? It did feel like magic."

Martha told the class, "I was on a road trip once when I noticed I was extremely low on gas. I started to get nervous. I could only see stretches of barren road ahead. It was getting dark, and I didn't know what I was going to do. Then just as my car started to putter out, I came upon a little gas station. It seemed to appear out of nowhere. The timing was perfect!"

Have you had a coincidence today?

What major coincidences have occurred in your life?

How do you define a coincidence?

To increase the coincidences in your life:
- Follow your heart and stay true to yourself.
- Expect more magic to come to you.
- Be open and aware in every situation.
- Ask for assistance from the universe.

## #5. Guiding Spirit Clues

I once was babysitting my friend's seven year old son, Evan. Evan's mother had passed away a year ago. He said to me, "I can't see Mommy, but I know she's here. "You do?" I asked him. "Oh yeah, I know she's here. It's just that now she's invisible." Have you ever felt that another spirit, someone who passed away, is guiding or watching over you? None of us are ever really alone. We are all being guided and protected by other spirits.

Here are some stories others have shared in my courses:

Sarina sensed her late uncle was near, "My uncle passed away five years ago, and I still miss him because we were so close. One day I was walking alone, thinking about him and how I felt he was still around. Then I looked down at the ground and there was a silver dollar. I couldn't believe it! He used to give me a silver dollar every time I'd see him."

Peter found his friend in a dream, "One of my close friends had passed away. We had some trouble before he died, and I felt terrible guilt about it. Then I had a dream about him. It was so vivid. He appeared to me and said, 'It's okay.' When I woke up I felt the burden lifted, and I felt that the dream was real."

Sherrie felt her late husband hug her, "I was lying on the couch just thinking about Bruce. Then I started to feel his presence. I felt him around just like I felt when he was alive. Then he hugged me! It's like he was hugging my heart so hard I could barely breath. It felt wonderful! My sister called me in the middle of his visit, and I told her, Bruce is here, I'll call you later. It left me with such peace."

Some people feel guided by spirits who are not necessarily friends or relatives, but are people with whom they feel a connection. When singer Bob Dylan won a music award, he said throughout the making of his album, he felt as though the singer Buddy Holly was there in the studio too.

I get great inspiration from John Lennon, musician and artist, who passed away years ago. Even though I never met him, I feel his spirit whenever I tune into him. When I was driving to teach my very first Flirting With Spirituality course, I popped in a John Lennon tape to give me inspiration. I started singing out loud and thinking about him. Then magic happened.

All of a sudden I saw him, John Lennon, pop out of the trees from a side street ahead! He was jumping up with his arms high in the air, and he had a huge smile! He looked young and vibrant. He was larger than life! My heart stopped. For a split second, I felt like I was in a dream!

A blinked and took another look. Ah-ha, it was a giant full length picture of John Lennon painted on a white bus, an advertisement for a local radio station. But to me, it was more than just a moving billboard. It was a sign. It was the spirit of John cheering me on!

If you suspect other spirits are guiding, protecting, or inspiring you, you are right. Magic is often invisible.

Who do you think may be guiding you?


What makes you sense that?


How does your guide make you feel?


To communicate with our guides more often we can:
- Tune in to them, think about them.
- Talk out loud to them when you're alone.
- Imagine they are with us at all times.
- Keep pictures and/or objects around us that have a connection with them.

## #6 Event and Encounter Clues

Many years ago, I was in an unhealthy long distance relationship and it was affecting my self-esteem. I knew I should break up, but at the time I was too weak. Then a series of telling events occurred. Every time, I tried to visit this guy, something went wrong. First, I couldn't get my car started to go see him, so I had the car fixed. On my second attempt to leave, I pulled out of the driveway, drove right over a nail and blew my tire. The tire was easy to repair, but just when I went back on the road, it started storming so I couldn't leave. After trying to visit him three times with continued obstacles, I knew something was shouting to me, "Break-up!" I finally did.

The universe is always speaking to us. Every event, every encounter, is filled with secret messages. Your heart and instinct will tell you what the message means, just keep paying attention.

Tom's clue came in one phrase,
"I was sent out of state on an assignment to write an article. My plane was delayed and I had to wait at the airport for three hours. I ended up sitting next to a guy who changed my life with one statement. I told him about my dream to write a book, how I had been putting it off, but had saved enough to get started. He said, 'It's sounds to me like you're ready.' '...You're ready......,' those words ran in my head. His one comment was just what I needed to hear. When I returned from the trip, I left my job and happily worked on my book full time. His words were my green light."

Sometimes we are angels in someone else's event:

Kala told the class,
"I was in an airport bathroom washing my hands when two women walked in.
They looked upset. One woman told her friend, 'What am I going to do? I can't
believe I spilled this coffee all over my skirt! How am I going to fly all
soaked?' I had an extra pair of sweats in my carrying case, so I spoke up,
'Would you like a pair of sweatpants? These are old. I don't need them.' The
woman was elated. 'Oh, thank you! Thank you! I checked all my luggage. Our
flight is four hours. You're a lifesaver! You're an angel!' It was such a little thing
and it made me feel so good."

Jake was an angel too,
"I found a check on the ground during my morning jog, so I popped it in
the mail. It was no big deal. I had forgotten all about it. Two weeks later, I
had a horrible day at work, and I felt useless. Then the mail arrived and in
it was a heartfelt thank-you note beginning with, 'You answered my
prayers! I needed that check so badly. You are my hero!' It really cheered
me up."

Have you ever done a little thing for someone which meant a great deal to
them?

Has someone ever said a casual remark to you that felt like an important message?


What events have been turning points for you and why?


Increase event and encounter magic by:
- Being open to secret clues in all situations.
- Remembering you are an undercover angel.
- Recognize there are helpers all around you.
- Trusting your instincts.

Clue review: feelings, signs, our innervoice, coincidences, guiding spirits, events, encounters and anything that you decide hold clues to finding and spreading joy.

Embrace the magic treasure hunt!

Here are a few more ways:

### Five Ways To Gain From Every Event And Encounter:

**1.** If you keep running into someone, start talking to them. You are encountering them for a reason. The message will come out and may lead to further coincidences.

Janet, who had just started her own interior decorating business, attended my class and later called me to share her exciting coincidence. "I went to the post office and waited in line. The woman in front of me turned around and smiled. I remember thinking she seems so nice. Next I went to the printing store and there she was again! We giggled when we saw each other. This time I smiled and said, 'This is so funny. I just took this course which says if you keep running into someone, talk to them. So Hi!, I'm Janet.' And she said, ' I believe that too, I'm Helen.' We shook hands and started chatting. Two weeks later, she ended up hiring me to decorate her house, and referred me to three more clients!"

Have you ever run into someone more than once?

**2.** Encounters can also be symbolic messages. Be aware of the meaning or symbol woven in the event.

Maria, from class, explained how a double encounter changed her awareness. "I was jogging around my neighborhood thinking about everything I had to do that day, which was a lot! So I started to get nervous and ran faster to get home. Then I jogged by this older woman who was wearing the same sweater I had on. That caught my attention. Then I noticed how happy and peaceful she looked and how she just was strolling along, taking her time. I envied her. I wanted to stop being in a hurry and stroll too. I was always hurrying. I walked the rest of the way home and it felt great! A week later, I was at the store rushing once more. Then I saw the same woman! Again, she was so in the moment, so calm. I decided it was a sign that again I needed to slow down. I never spoke with her, but just her presence held a message.

Have you ever had a symbolic encounter?

**3.** Don't get discouraged. If you are really meant to talk to or see a specific person, you get much more than one chance. Life will serve them up to you until the message is delivered.

Brian told our class how he met his wife, "I went to a concert when I first moved to town. I met this wonderful woman who I spoke with for five minutes, but then her friends dragged her off. I was just kicking myself because I didn't get her number! Three months later I saw her drive by, but it was so quick and she didn't see me. I thought, it's just not meant to be. And then a month later I was in an elevator and there she was! This time I knew better. By the time we got to the fifteenth floor, I had her number!"

If you see someone that you wished you had spoken to but didn't, don't beat yourself up. Just say the magic words,

**"My next chance is coming at the right time."**

**4.** If a plan of yours falls through or something doesn't seem to work out, it's life's magic telling you something better is in store for you.

Gretta told our class, "I had my heart set on this one college. My best was friend was accepted, but I wasn't. So I went to my second choice, a smaller school. Now I'm glad I was turned down. My friend actually transferred to my school because our first choice had too many people. We ended up loving the smaller school!"

When my first book came out, one of my goals was to land an appearance on The Today Show. I sent my materials to the book segment producer, and I followed up with several phone calls. Finally, they called back to see my demo-tape. I'm almost there I thought! Then months passed and I heard nothing. I guess they didn't want me. I let it go.

Six months later, The Today Show called. It was a different producer, a series producer, who called me. He said he had seen me on another show and wanted to feature me in a Flirting series. I didn't even think of that possibility! Here I had been chasing after one segment, and I ended up with three segments over three days! Life had a much better plan.

Say the magic words,
**"Something much better is in store for me."**

Can you think of an instance where life served you up something much better than you hoped for?

**5.** When things seem to just "fall into place" it's the universe telling you: you are on the right track.

Gary told us in class, "I always wanted to quit my job and leave the city, but I was torn. I decided to take a weekend to think about it. So I took a drive to a small town a couple hours away. As soon as I was in the car, coincidences kept happening. First I was humming a Rolling Stones song when I started the car. Then I turned on the radio and it was on! While driving, I became real hungry and thought, I'd love a huge chocolate shake right now. Just as I thought that, I saw a sign that said 'Dairy Queen Next Exit.' I found a hotel and went in thinking, I'm going to sleep like a king. Then when I registered, the clerk said, 'We have a special deal tonight. You can have the King Suite at regular room price.' Why is all this quick luck happening? I thought to myself on the way to dinner. The Hostess who greeted me was so friendly. I said to her, 'You're in a good mood tonight.' And she said 'You bet! My husband and I just moved here a month ago from the city. We love it!' That was my final coincidence. I received the message. I moved out of the city and moved to that nice town two months later."

When have a series of lucky coincidences happened to you?

Now that we've covered the various clues and how to feel connected to them, let's talk about.....

## How To Ask For Clues

If you're confused about something or need help with a problem or goal, all you have to do is ask for help.

Just think it, "I need a sign" or say it out loud, "I need assistance."

Then pay open attention, listen with patience for clues, trust the process and your answer will come,

guaranteed.


Do you have a special way of asking for help?

## The Power Of Declaration

The magic flows within you and all around you. Just as the universe is responding to your inner desires, you are guiding it with your thoughts, words and actions. Whatever it is that you want to be, say I AM.

One woman in my course explained, "When I started my own catering business, things were very slow at first, and I wasn't helping. To myself I would say, " Maybe I'm not cut out to be entrepreneur. And when people would ask me, 'How's business?' I'd say, 'Well, I'm trying.' I came so close to quitting so many times. Then I turned to the power of declaration. First I took out a piece of paper and wrote, 'I am a successful caterer. I am busy with three accounts a week. I am making a profit. I am happy and I am making my customers happy too.' Just reading it and imagining it made me feel hopeful. I left the house that day and ran into an old friend. When she asked, 'How's business?' I proudly said, 'Terrific! I am so happy.' "That's great" she said, Do you have time to cater a party for me this weekend?" It worked instantly. Now I start my days with declarations!"

How do you sound when you talk to yourself?

Here are some sample solution I AM's from some of my classes:

| Former Self-talk | New Declaration |
|---|---|
| I have so much stress. | I am handling things one step at a time. |
| I always tell white lies, and I can't stand it. | I am committed to honesty in every moment. |
| I'm lost. | I am drawing everything I need right to me. |
| I'm so insecure. | I am loved. |
| I want to go after my dream, but I'm scared. | I am living my dream and thriving. |
| Everything was happening so quickly, why did it slow down? | I trust life's magic cycle. |
| I wish I made a difference. | I am a leader. |

(add some of your own)

## I Am

Use your I am declarations to cut a fear thought right off. That means whenever you begin to hear yourself say anything fearful, anything, replace it instantly with "I am." It starts to become a habit, then an imprint, then reality!

Here are three I am statements I did just this morning:

"What if I don't finish this book by my goal date?!"
(cut!)
"I am right on schedule."


"I hope Dad gets the card I sent him."
(cut!)
"I am sure Dad has the card right now."


"MMMM. I look bloated today."
(cut!)
"I am healthy and happy."

Recipes For Instant Magic
**"Universal magic is guiding me."**

Say the above statement every day as much as you would like. Say it while you're driving, showering, walking and waiting. Let the universe know you are tuned in and receiving. Say it, and the magic flows to you even faster.

Here are some more recipes to choose from:

-I am being guided by universal forces.

-I am being guided to my highest purpose.

-I am magic.

-I am being guided at the right place at the right time.

-I am being granted everything I desire.

-I am drawing what I need right to me.

-I am filled with optimism.


Your turn:

-I am


-I am

## The Power Of Repetition

Every thought we have makes an imprint, which spreads through our bodies, spirits and the world around us. When we continually think negatively about ourselves or a situation, that sends a toxic message that ripples outward.

Repeating our "I am" declarations increases our power immediately and magnifies the magic we draw to ourselves. Make it a habit. Imprint your best possible self.

Our thoughts are our greatest tool and can change an outcome in an instant.

# The Power of Tuning In

In the center of yourself, is a calm place that receives all the answers you need.

It's kind of like your own library. It's filled with endless knowledge and information about you.

When we want to enter that place, we need to be quiet and clear our minds, allowing the answers to float in.

Here are some ways people have entered their internal library.

- I take a walk alone.
- I turn off the phone and the TV and I sit in my favorite chair and look out the window.
- I lay on my bed and listen to nature sounds.
- I take a nice long, warm bath.
- I get a massage and let my mind drift.
- I take a day trip away.
- I refrain from speaking one day, once a month.
- I give myself 15 extra minutes each morning to lay in bed and think.
- I go to the lake and watch the water.
- I move to music.

What are some ways you enter your library?

## Unleash Your Psychic Within

Bernie, a stockbroker who attended my class, made a discovery, "I never thought I had any psychic ability. Even when I heard the word psychic, I pictured someone with a crystal ball. One Sunday afternoon, I was watching a basketball game on TV, and I was totally engrossed in it. I started to notice that every time someone attempted a shot, I could predict if he would make a basket or not. I guessed right three times in a row so I just kept concentrating and guessed five more correctly. The next day, I started trying this method at work. When I was looking at stocks to invest, in addition to doing my usual research, I also tried to focus inward and get a sense of the outcome. It made a big difference for my business and actually for all my decision making. I guess I am kind of psychic after all."

We can always recognize an emotional reaction because it sounds and feels fearful, urgent and panic-filled. A psychic response is the opposite. It sounds and feels peaceful, enlightened and calm. Everyone of us has psychic powers. All we have to do is tune in, focus, calm our minds and feel the answer.

When have you felt especially psychic?

Before we move on, let's take a quick review of Awareness:

 *Life is a magical treasure hunt filled with clues.

 *Clues are: feelings, signs, spirits, events, innervoice,
      coincidences, encounters and more.

 *Be open to clues at all times and the magic increases.

 *Decipher clues with your instincts.

 *When you need help, just ask.

 *Declaring I am brings instant power and universal response.

 *Tune into your internal library for answers.

 *You are naturally psychic.


Be open.

Be aware.

Find the magic treasure.

**Gratitude:**
**Everything happens for a reason.**

**Give thanks and feel instant energy.**

Imagine you are starring in your own movie. You are the lead character and every other character in the film and every plot twist is there to help your character grow. Some parts of the plot are scary, some are suspenseful, some are hilarious.

You really are the star of you own movie, your life. Everything in your life happens for a reason. When we grasp the meaning and gift of every situation, we magnify our magic and create instant energy.

## Everything Happens For A Reason

Everything that happens in life from major events to momentary encounters are filled with meaning. We magnify our power by the way in which we respond to each situation. All we have to do is ask ourselves three magic questions:

**Why did I create this situation?** One magical quality of life is that we are constantly drawing to us the lessons that we need to learn. We empower our spirit by asking this question and seeking the lesson inside.

Judith, from my seminar, explained, "I was a high power attorney and mother of three. One day I woke up with exhaustion and couldn't get out of bed. At first I panicked and complained, 'Why me?' But as time passed, I learned why. The breakdown was just what I needed to see how I had been living, filled with stress, constantly busy, and constantly worried. After several months of recuperating and soul searching, I came through the exhaustion a much wiser and enlightened person. I realized I had brought this upon myself, and I changed my whole routine and pace of my life. I can see now the breakdown was a total blessing."

**What am I learning from this?** The moment we grasp the lesson is the moment our magic and power intensifies.

Betty explained, "I set two of my friends up on a blind date and the next thing I knew I was in the middle of their squabble. I started to beat myself up for making the date in the first place, and I was growing impatient with their behavior. Then I asked that question, 'What I am learning from this?' And I knew, I'll never get in the middle again. This declaration of boundaries made me feel much better and I've stayed out of their business ever since.

**How will I handle something like this in the future?** Every moment prepares us for the next. By examining the lesson and forming a plan, we immediately strengthen our power.

LeRoy told the class, "I once lent a good friend a pretty substantial amount of money and it destroyed our friendship. It was painful, but it was worth it. I made a commitment to myself at that point that I had learned my lesson and I would never do that again. Last week, in fact, an associate asked for a loan and I felt so grateful to have an experience to draw from. I told him, 'Tell you what, I'll help you make money, but I won't lend it,' and I felt great."

Are you going through a difficult or confusing situation right now? Have you just come out of one? Ask yourself these three magic questions:

1.Why did I create this situation?

2. What am I learning from it?

3. How will I handle something like this in future?

## The Truth Is Magic!

| Illusion | Truth |
|---|---|
| Life is out to get me, I can't take it. | Life is teaching me lessons, I am strong. |
| Events are always random. | Everything happens for a reason. |
| I regret so much. | I understand the choices I made based on what I knew and needed to learn. |
| I wasted my time. | I needed the experience to grow. |
| I must control everything. | Letting go brings things to me. |
| I have a bad history. | I am new in this moment. |

## Some Reasons Take Time To Emerge

If we ever grow discouraged because we can't find the reason, all we have to do is tell ourselves, "The story is still unfolding." The lesson will always emerge. I'm just figuring out why I experienced a certain incident when I was sixteen. I had just received my drivers license and my mom had lent me her car, a big green Buick. Each day when I'd arrive home from school, my father would be waiting for me, directing me so that I would back into the carport correctly.

One day when I arrived home, I was thinking more about my upcoming test, than backing in, and despite my father's frantic stop signal, I drove through the porch! "YOU-ARE-GROUNDED-YOU-WILL-PAY-FOR-THIS-I'M-GOING-TO-TAKE-A-TIME-OUT," my dad managed to communicate through clenched teeth. I went to my room and sulked over my error.

The next day in school we were assigned to write about a difficult thing that had happened to us this year. With the gashed up porch still fresh in my mind, I told my horror story. But as I wrote it, I saw how funny it was- kind of like an I LOVE LUCY episode. At that moment, I fell in love with writing and storytelling. I decided to pursue writing and speaking because of that paper. And that means I am an author and speaker today because when I was sixteen, I drove through the porch!

When we can't find the lesson, remember the magic spell:
**"The story is unfolding."**

Here are some ways others calm themselves in a stressful moment:

-I take three long deep breaths.

-I imagine I'm sitting on a cloud watching myself from above.

-I remind myself of the truth: everything always works out.

-I repeat, I am calm.

-I try to be alone and silent for ten minutes.

-I stretch.

-I focus on relaxing all the muscles in my body.

-I draw.

-I imagine a white light is pouring through my body.

-I meditate.

-I pray.

-I play with my cat.

-I chant.

-I watch clouds pass.

What are ways you calm yourself when you feel stressed?

## Everything Goes In Cycles

Everything in life is a magic cycle. And just like the change of seasons, one cycle helps us appreciate another. Here is some wisdom from other spiritual artists, like you and me, who embrace the magical cyclical process.

David, a sales representative, explained to the class, "I've been selling for fifteen years and it's all about cycles. Whenever I get a series of no's or rejections in a row, I never get discouraged because I know the yes's are coming."

Jennifer, an aspiring actress, then added, "That's so true! When I first went into acting, I couldn't believe how many parts I landed my first year. I thought it would just keep going and then the second year everything slowed down. I remember feeling disappointed, but it ended up being the best thing for me. I used that year to study my craft and work on my self-esteem. It really wasn't a slow year, it was a grow year. And wouldn't you know it? The following year things grew busy again, and I was much more prepared and more skilled to handle it."

Peter, a teacher, explained, "The cycles of life give us balance. Just yesterday one of my second graders said, 'It's hard being sad, but then I really know when I'm happy!'"

What cycles do you see in your life?

What messages do they send you?

<u>Life's Magic Trick: Mistakes are Miracles Waiting To Happen</u>

Life is filled with magic tricks and one of them is that mistakes are really just miracles waiting to happen.

The creation of my family name held such magic.
Over hundreds of years ago, in a small town outside of Frankfurt Germany, a family named Meyer, (some of my oldest relatives) lived on top of the town's central hill. One day Dad Meyer bought his family a special present- a large, new "spiegel!" (In German, mirror is called spiegel.) As Meyer climbed the hill, he made sure he was extra careful.

He finally reached the front door, but with sadness and frustration, he discovered the mirror wouldn't fit through the doorway. Feeling defeated, he left the mirror outside and leaned it against the house.

"Der spiegel! Der spiegel!" The next thing he knew, crowds of people were gathered at the bottom of the hill. The mirror reflected the sun and the Meyer house was shining like a huge, brilliant diamond, spreading light and joy to the entire village! As villagers and tourists passed by, they'd stop and point at the sighting, delightfully shouting, "Der spiegel! Der spiegel!"

And that's how the Spiegel name was miraculously created.
For Meyer, what started as a goof, ended up as greatness.

Everything happens for a reason -
Mistakes are simply miracles on their way.


When has a "mistake" worked in your favor?


Can you see a miracle coming through a problem right now?



How do you talk to yourself when you make a "mistake?"

Expressing Gratitude: The Instant Energy Miracle

Something powerful happens within ourselves the moment we say
"thanks." We fill ourselves with strength and purpose receiving instant
energy and increasing our magic.

In the following pages we will explore 8 ways to express our gratitude and
magnify our power. (And remember these are just a few possible ways.
You the artist, you may have 18 more of you own!)

## #1. Give Thanks In Advance

When you have a wish, the best way to insure it's fruition is to thank the universe in advance for granting it. Our internal faith activates a response, putting our wish in instant motion.

Try it. You can feel it working immediately in your spirit. Think of a wish you have. A new job? Meeting a soulmate? Anything as long as it doesn't hurt anyone and is in your best interests.

Now imagine the wish has been granted. Picture how it looks and makes you feel. Hold the feeling and vision for a moment. You can literally feel it happening now!

Now say, "Thank you universe for granting me this wish."

That's all it takes. Magic is very simple.
Now all you have to do is hold the faith that the
wish is granted.

Your wish is magically traveling to you.

## #2. Remember The Magic Slogan "I've put in on the order"

Making a wish is a lot like ordering at a restaurant. You give your order. The waitress (or waiter) brings it to the kitchen and you patiently wait for the food to come.

Usually she brings the small requests, like your drink or your water, right away. Life works that way too. Small wishes often come true quickly. And big wishes, the main course size, take a little more time.

Whenever we find ourselves wondering, "When is it going to happen?" or "Should I make the wish again?"
We need to remind ourselves:

**"I've put in the order. It will emerge at the right time. The universe is magic and has perfect timing."**

## #3. Embrace Every Single Emotion And Feeling You Have

Tim, a class participant, told me, "Jill, I want to be spiritual, but I get angry a lot. I guess I have a long way to go." That's a misconception. No feelings are wrong or bad. They are a precious part of who we are and a gift from the universe. Spirituality is about accepting and nurturing our feelings from anger to freedom. To be truly spiritual is to be in touch with our feelings, to express them, and to embrace all facets of our human experience.

Amy explained to the class how she learned from her feelings: "I grew up in a household where I felt I wasn't loved or listened to. This really hurt me and soon I started to scream or act out to get attention. And my parents would say, 'Stop your anger...you're so negative!' This only made me more hurt, angry and completely ashamed of myself. I carried my anger with me to adulthood feeling so badly every time I lashed out. Then one day I yelled at a co-worker and I felt terrible afterward.

But a miracle happened. Instead of blaming me, she said, 'You seem so hurt and upset. What can I do?' I was shocked. She reached out to me with such acceptance and warmth. She knew my anger was a cry for help.

I've learned that my anger is pain expressed and a need for love. I am working on loving myself better everyday. Now I examine my feelings first, instead of yelling. I realize all my feelings are an important signal of where I've been and a link to how I want to nurture and re-create myself today."

Feel your feelings.
Listen to them.
Nurture them.
Express them.

Living Dishonestly Wounds Our Spirit

Being Honest Heals Our Spirit

## #4. Send Positive Messages With Your Eyes

Whenever we look at someone, they can feel our thoughts. We are all connected through a magical tapestry. Thinking kindly of someone ripples outward to the world and back through ourselves.

One wonderfully silent and powerful way to express gratitude is to make a sincere habit of thinking the nicest thought possible when we notice anybody or look in someone's eyes.

A nice thought is never pity, but appreciation and compassion. Nate explained, "I saw a homeless woman and as I passed her, I looked in her eyes and thought, you are a very strong person. She smiled at me and said, 'Good morning!' I felt as though she heard me! It was such a little moment, but it changed me. I want to give more."

To notice the beauty in every being is a huge expression of gratitude. And like magic, it works instantly!

## #5.Establish Your Boundaries

Personal boundaries are the lines we draw to protect ourselves. When we take care of those needs, we are thanking the universe and increasing our magic power. Drawing our boundaries is not about hurting others, but about honoring our spirit.

We need to draw boundaries with others when:
-We feel invaded.
-We feel taken advantage of.
-We feel disrespected.
-We sense dishonesty.
-We feel uncomfortable.

When we stay committed to our self-respect, we magically draw respect. We teach others how to treat us.

"I vow to always nurture and respect my spirit."

_____

(sign here)

### #6. Embrace Your Healing Power

One wonderful gift the universe has given all of us is the magical power to heal. The more we appreciate that power and embrace it, the more healed we feel ourselves. It's simple too!

Here are some ways others use their unique healing power:

- I'm a good listener. Whenever I give someone empathy, they just light up.
- I love to laugh! I heal myself and others by laughing long and hard when someone is being funny.
- I pretend I'm an undercover angel. I donate half my earnings to charity, anonymously.
- I like to be silly. When people are being too serious, I get goofy. It always melts the tension.
- I'm calm. I've found I can calm others just by keeping my composure when they're upset.
- I love to dream big. I see how grateful people are when I use my dreaming to encourage them, "You can do it. I can see it now!"
- I love to walk. I always bring a plastic bag with me and pick up litter along the way.
- I love animals. I take in foster pets until they find a home.
- I'm a positive person. People appreciate my energy.

Now it's your turn. What magical healing gifts do you have?

### #7. Show Thanks By Living In Non-Judgement

When we judge ourselves and others, we are doubting the magic of life. By accepting ourselves and others, we have faith that everything happens for a reason including where and who we are in each moment.

Mimi explained,
"I didn't even realize how much I was judging others until I decided not to judge anyone, including myself, for just one day. Any time I'd jump to a criticism or assumption of someone, I catch myself and replace my thoughts with compassion and an open mind. This felt so right I did it another day, and then the next day. My new habit felt so good inside, I didn't realize it was helping me physically. I just learned that since I stopped judging, my blood pressure went down!"

The Non-Judgement Vow: "I am not perfect. I accept others are not perfect. We are all equal and special in our own way. I embrace myself and others for who we are in this moment, which is exactly where we need to be. Life has a magical plan."

_____

(sign here)

## **#8.** Shift from "Why not?" To "What is!"

One of the greatest benefits of gratitude is that it magically and instantly frees us from needing. Needing something so badly creates a trap. We become prisoners of our own desires as we attach our happiness to something outside of ourselves. Gratitude fills us from within.

William explained, "My whole life I had a goal to be famous in my field. I worked and worked to make a name for myself and no matter what I achieved along the way, it wasn't enough. I had to reach that fame. I married a wonderful woman and had two beautiful children and still I felt pain over the fact that my goal wasn't accomplished. I would find myself being incredibly jealous of anyone else that was in my eyes 'ahead of me.' I'd agonize, why not me?!

Then one day my wife brought home a puppy and my six year old daughter said, 'Oh! I think we are the luckiest family in the whole world!' I felt ashamed. She was so alert and so grateful, and I was so closed, still chasing an illusion. When the kids went to sleep that night, I made a list of everything good in my life. I thought about what the fame really represented to me: importance, power, proof that I mattered. How ironic, I have that right at home, right now.

I stopped worrying about being famous and started embracing what I had. I was finally free."

I am grateful for: (make your list)

Great job on Gratitude, let's review:

    *Everything happens for a reason.

    *Mistakes are miracles waiting to happen.

    *Giving thanks brings instant energy.

    *Some reasons and wishes take time, give thanks in advance.

    *Everything in life is a cycle.

    *Send positive messages with your eyes.

    *Establish your boundaries and embrace your feelings.

    *Be liberated through non-judgement.

    *Shift from why not to what is.

Being grateful makes you great full.

Imagine:
Thoughts are real.


Imagine the best for yourself and others.

Imagine you are a superhero. You have a special power that makes you soar to success and help others around you. That power is your imagination. You know that in order to accomplish your goals, all you have to do is use your mind.

You are that superhero and your imagination is all powerful. We all have the mind power to make anything happen. Everything starts with a thought, an idea that ripples outward and manifests into reality.

## Everything Begins With A Seed Of Thought

Everything starts with a thought......everything. Before anything becomes reality, it first appears in our mind. Even when we daydream, we are igniting a process that puts our thoughts into action. If we can see it, we can be it.

The most important event in my life began with a casual daydream. When I moved to Minneapolis, I made a new friend, Beth, who introduced me to her younger brother, Joe. She said, "He's coming to visit me from college, in Arizona. He's very entrepreneurial, like you. Come to lunch with us!"

Beth was right. Joe was very much like me. He was earning his business degree and dreamed one day of having his own company to produce products that combined education and entertainment. "Education and entertainment?!" I gasped, "I want to be a motivational entertainer. Hey you could manage me. We could be business partners!" We giggled.

We stayed friendly (just friends) throughout his college career, after which he moved to Duluth, a town nearby. One day he came passing through town and stopped by to say "Hi." One year later we were married. We have our own motivational entertainment company called Goal Getters, where Joe is my partner and manager.

To this day we reminisce about our magical first "meeting," where we didn't even realize we were planting a seed of thought that came true six years later!

Whatever we think about, we draw right to us.

Plant a thought seed today.

## Thoughts Heal

Studies show that people who are prayed for heal faster, proof that we all are gifted with magic powers that heal.

Mary, from my course, recalled, "My aunt, who I adore, was very ill in intensive care. She had internal infections and the doctors said it was touch and go. I wanted my aunt to be well so badly. I shut my eyes and imagined I was standing at the foot of her bed. I pretended I saw a healing white light covering her feet. 'Look Aunt Ann,' I smiled. 'The white light is embracing you and it's healing you, look!' I imagined we were giggling and marveling over the magic light that slowly moved all the way to the top of her head. 'It's at you knees!' I'd cheer, and she'd say, 'Now it's on my stomach!' I just sat there with my eyes shut and pictured this scenario with all my heart and focus. Minutes passed. When I opened my eyes, I couldn't believe how much better I felt. I was trying to heal my aunt and yet it ended up helping me!

Two days later I found out Aunt Ann was making a full recovery. I went to visit her the next week and the moment I walked in the room she said, 'I had a dream about you!'"

Can you think of someone you care about who needs healing?

Imagine them being healed right now.

You have just made magic.

## Thoughts Travel

Have you ever seen the wind?
The wind itself is invisible.
We can feel it. We can watch it move the trees,
but we can not actually see the wind.
Still, we know it is a very real energy.


Thoughts are just like the wind.
They are an invisible real energy that travels.
Thoughts can feel like hurricanes or warm breezes.
All energy travels, and energy never dies.


Every mind creates the world. Every thought counts.

Can you see your soul? Your feelings?
We are made up of energy too.

## Imagine The Best Possible Future For Everybody

Here are a few simple and effective ways to change the world:

- Nurture your own spirit and bring harmony to all your relationships.
- Tell people you know in your heart things are getting better and better everyday.
- Here are some ways others have responded when asked "How do you know things are getting better?":

" I believe we each create the future. So I'm visualizing the brightest future possible and I can see it manifesting.

" I can feel it's better. There is a spiritual revolution happening right now."

" There is just too much goodness in life to think otherwise."

" I see that everything evolves. So as a world, I believe our souls are evolving too and we are getting smarter and wiser."

What are other ways we can project a positive future?

Hope leads to happening!

## An Exercise To Set A Thought In Motion:

Take a moment and imagine your life one year from now. What do you want to have happened? Imagine it and hold that image for a few seconds.

In the designated space below write down the date one year from now. Now make a list of everything you want to happen, but write it in the past tense. For example. If you want to have all your closets cleaned by next year, write, "I cleaned out all my closets."

Here are some samples from past participants:
- I left my job and found a great new one!
- I met a wonderful person who has all the qualities I'm looking for!
- I grew so calm and filled with faith.
- I won the songwriting contest I entered!

Your list:
The year is_____ .

   -I


   -I


   -I

Now once you've written it down, (feel free to be as detailed as you'd like,) share your list with a friend. You could go beyond just reading the list out loud. Be creative, describe the events: "I felt so great when I found this job. It happened so fast! Here's what I did to land that interview."

Notice how exhilarating it feels to "live" these dreams. Your spirit is joyful. It's already working.

Now take it one step further. How have these happenings affected your life movie? What will your life look like?

Here's what other course participants have added to their lists:
-I left my job and found a new one!
  I wake up every morning excited for the day. I feel so fulfilled and respected. I'm proud of myself for making the change.
-I won the songwriting contest I entered! I am filled with confidence. I create new art every day.

Your turn:
-I


-I


-I


Save this list and read it every day or as often as you like.
Fill your thoughts with positive expectancy.


You are casting a magic spell!

## Mindmelding

My husband and I have been married and working partners for several years. We often have simultaneous thoughts. We'll be working in separate rooms, and one of us will come visit the other to share an idea, only to hear, "I was just thinking about that too!" Our minds and thoughts have grown so in sync that we joke to each other, "Next time we're apart, send me a secret message."

One time I went for a walk alone when Joe was out at a meeting. I left him a note and went to the lake. Halfway around, I started to feel like someone was right behind me, literally a step behind me. I kept turning around but no one was there. The feeling stayed with me.

Finally, I turned around again, and looked way in the distance. About a mile away I saw a tiny figure. I waited for it to get a little more in view. There was Joe! We jogged to each other and caught up giggling. I told him, "I thought someone was right behind me! Joe smiled and said, "Yep! I was sending you a mind message!"

Have your ever mindmelded with someone else?

Have you ever read somebody's thoughts?

Has someone ever read yours?

## Thoughts Heal Relationships

If you are having trouble with a friend, relative or co-worker, your thoughts can help heal the turmoil. Just follow this simple two step plan.

Step 1.
Imagine what needs to happen to support your spirit. Depending on the situation, you can imagine:

- harmony and respect between the two of you, or

- an open and gentle discussion, or

- separating on good terms, or

- whatever you feel needs to take place.

Step 2. Be ready with a plan.

Imagine what ways you can behave in order to help create this desired outcome, while still taking care of your spirit. Sometimes your thoughts will travel so fast you won't need to use the plan.

J.D. explained, "Every year at Thanksgiving my older cousin gives me grief about my girlfriends. I imagined that this year, it would be different, and I had a plan to tell him how uncomfortable he made me feel if it happened again. I couldn't believe it, but when I did see him this year, he didn't even bring it up! My mind message worked."

Other times you may need the plan which works in combination with your thoughts.

For example, a woman in my course wanted harmony with a difficult co-worker. She imagined how she would behave and what she would say in order to create harmony and protect herself.

Veronica told us, "I made a plan that when I see Cindy at the office, I will smile and walk by. If she stops to give me more unwanted advice, I will say warmly and gently, 'I appreciate your concern, but I don't need any advice. I feel great about my life.' Just having a plan made me feel better. In the meantime, I tried to imagine Cindy and I getting along well.

When Monday came, I saw Cindy coming down the hall. I smiled and remembered my plan. 'Veronica! Nice dress, you'd look even better if it was pink,' she said. I gave my planned response and walked away. I felt strong, and I continued to imagine harmony between us.

The next day when I saw her, a miracle happened. She approached me and apologized for her past behavior. 'Veronica, when you said you were happy with your life, it really made me think. I've been unhappy and have been projecting my problems on you and so many others. I'm going to stop giving unwanted advice and work on myself. I'm sorry I was so rude.' We've been on great terms ever since."

Are there any relationships in your life that need healing?

Step 1. Imagine what needs to happen to protect your spirit.

Step 2. What's your plan?

## Thoughts Heal Old Wounds

Sometimes relationships end on difficult terms leaving us feeling guilty or angry. We can heal our wounds immediately with three magic thoughts.

In your mind and heart,

1. Thank this person for what you learned about yourself by knowing them.

2. Acknowledge exactly what you gained from the experience.

3. Wish this person wisdom and enlightenment and release the past from your thoughts.

Flora, from my course, commented on her healing, "I had a dysfunctional off and on romance many years ago. Even though I had not spoken with this guy since it ended, I still felt so angry about it. In my mind I would replay our conversations and recall all the abusive things he would say to me. It was like living it all over again. I would get headaches just thinking about it! I tried the three step plan.

1. Thank you _____ for being a pivotal relationship in my life. When I decided to go out with you, my self-esteem was low. At that time, I believed I deserved to be mistreated.

2. What I gained from the experience in the long run was a new sense of self-power.

3. I wish you wisdom and enlightenment and I release you and myself from the past."

What needs healing in your life right now?

Take a moment and do the three step plan.

Great Job! Let's review Imagine:

* Thoughts are made of real energy.
* Everything that exists started with a thought.
* Daydreaming has secret power.
* Our thoughts travel and ripple through us.
* Direct your future by imagining it.
* Thoughts heal relationships. Imagine harmony and have a plan.
* Projecting a positive future in your mind helps the world.
* Every thought is creative, you are an artist.

When we pay attention to our spirit,
use our mind power,
and embrace our connection with everything,

miracles happen.

**Connect:**
**Magic Is everywhere.**


**Reach out - Life joyfully reaches back.**

Imagine you are an artistic magician and the universe is your personal assistant. When you have a desire, you create your own artistic spells and your assistant is always there to help you, guide you, and remind you of your power.

You really are that magician and the universe works with you. By reaching out and connecting, you make magic everywhere and you create joy.

## Your Spirituality Is Your Magic Art

One time I was babysitting for my friend's nine year old daughter, Clare. After we listened to some records and played three rounds of hide and go seek, we were thinking of what to do next when Clare said, "I know! Wait, first I have to get something!" She excitedly ran back to the kitchen and came back with two pieces of cheese. She handed me a piece and explained the next game, "OK. Let's pretend we're stranded on this desert island and the only food we have is this cheese!"

And the game had started. We sat on the floor and slowly rationed our cheese as we thought of ways to escape the island. Halfway through the cheese, we started talking about all the things we missed back home and how much we love our family. We laughed a lot and shared our favorite stories, which gave each other strength. Clare told me, "If the island gets cold, you can wear my sweater."

By the time we finished the cheese, we saw an imaginary plane coming to rescue us! As we boarded, I thought about my island experience and how it helped me feel so grateful for what I have. I was also thankful for this time with Clare, who showed me her special way of embracing life's magic.

One of the most liberating aspects of flirting with spirituality is that it frees us to connect with the magic in our way, our style. Our creativity is our greatest gift. In the following pages, we'll explore ways in which others have connected. Use these ideas to inspire you to make your own spiritual art.

See The World Through A Child's Eyes


imagine,


play,


pretend.

## Tune Into Nature

Whenever I walk outside, I immediately feel more alert and alive, don't you? Nature is calming, exhilarating and healing all at once. We find our spirits lifted just by spending time with the most magical part of Earth that connects with the magic inside of us. Here are some ways other people in my courses have tuned into nature:

- I love to be with nature, a system that works perfectly on it's own and teaches me to trust the natural process of life.

- When I feel stressed or overworked, I love to go to this park and sit by my favorite tree. Everything in the park is so calm and quiet, helping me to slow down and listen within. The tree is like an old friend: calm, strong and still. Sometimes I keep so busy by "doing." The tree teaches me to just "be."

- Nature teaches me to embrace the diversity in life. All the different flowers, plants and animals help me appreciate the differences and uniqueness in each person, each culture.

- I love the sound of water. It fills me with an instant calm. I sit by the lake for hours and listen to the quiet waves."

- I collect rocks and crystals. I use them to heal everything from my headache to a burn. My friend had a sore knee and I held my rocks and crystal on it and told her she was healing. The next day her pain was gone!

- Nature to me holds all of life's answers. It shows me that everything is interconnected and moves in cycles, just like life.

Go flirt with nature.

## Everyone Is An Artist

In the beginning of this book, I mentioned that since I was little, I felt everything around me was alive. I would see spirit faces in elements of nature like the clouds and the trees. Even today when I stare at a cloud or look into the woods, I see little faces emerge. It's creative and comforting to make art out of anything. Here are some comments from some past course participants, spiritual artists like you and me.

Marty looks for faces too,
"I see faces in wood. I take pieces of beautiful sanded wood and draw faces upon the natural faces in the wood. I paint the outline of the faces in and give these pieces as gifts to my friends and family."

Kurt looks out the window,
"I look out my telescope at night and play connect the stars. I love to spot shapes and symbols."

Brent goes for a ride,
"I love to go bike riding and find new routes and new streets. I feel like an adventurer."

Sandra goes to her garden,
"Gardening to me is my spiritual art. I lose track of time when I'm working in my garden. I love being outside working with the earth. I find the plants and flowers and every aspect of it completely creative and healing."

What ways can you make art out of the world around you?

# Connect With Animals

Whenever I see a bird fly, I feel like I'm flying too. Just a few moments of watching a bird spread it's wings and glide, takes my breath away, and my spirit soars along in flight. Animals are a magical part of nature. They heal us, inspire us and give us love. For many of us, connecting with animals brings us a profound sense of wonder and joy. Here are some comments from other spiritual artists who feel the magic of animals:

"My dog is my therapist. He always listens to me and trusts that I can solve my own problems."

"We had the most uptight office climate. Then my boss started bringing in his dog, Duke. Duke changed everything. People felt happier and more relaxed with him around. We all got more work done too. Duke is now on staff permanently. I think every office should have a dog."

"Petting my cat is very meditative for me. I feel so calm and appreciated."

"Whenever I see a bird or butterfly, I feel like I live in Disney cartoon. My heart jumps."

"Sometimes I feel like I have telepathy with my horse."

"When I start to get a big ego, I come home to my Golden Retriever who reminds me what really counts. He loves me for me. He could care less about my job title or how my hair looks. He humbles me."

If you don't have a pet, you can still benefit form animal power. Just observe and appreciate the animals you do see. If you visit a friend who has a pet, spend some time with it. Animals have magic healing power.

Animal are:

in touch with their spirit

creative

expressive

full of wonder

curious

honest and direct

always loving

our teachers.

## Creative Daydreaming

Daydreaming is one of our most powerful and creative art forms. Our mind is an infinite palette of possibilities and our daydreams make a magical imprint, the first step to our dreams coming true.

Everything that has happened in my career started with a daydream. When I published my first book I wanted to be on The Oprah Winfrey Show so badly. Almost everyday, I'd imagine myself on her stage. I even had my outfit picked out. For two years I sent in pitches, and I visualized my appearance in full detail. Then one day the phone call came, "I've been expecting you!" I told the producers. They booked me as an expert for a full hour, and I was ready. It was such an incredible experience! Daydreaming makes everything fall into place.

I kept daydreaming.

Later in my career I was auditioning for my own weekly advice segment "Dear Jill" on an existing national television show. For my audition, I went on the show for two segments and answered viewer questions on the spot. When I came home the day of my audition, I put the tape of my appearance in the video machine, and turned the sound way down. Then I put the tape on slow motion and put on my favorite Beatles music. I made my own music video, watching myself perform to the Beatles and dreaming of my own segment. A week later I found out I landed the job and like magic, the producers edited my first "Dear Jill" feature to the Beatles! I saw my daydream come true before my eyes!

Here are some other examples of creative daydreaming from other spiritual artists:

"I wanted to get into better shape. I took a picture of my face and taped it to a picture of a much stronger body and taped it on my bedroom wall. I went on a sensible exercise plan and looked at the picture everyday for motivation. Six months later I took the dream picture down, replacing it with the new me."

"I draw a comic storyboard of something I want to happen."

"I put on my favorite classical music and imagine it's the soundtrack to my life. I close my eyes and see my goals and triumphs like I was watching myself in a movie. It gets me so hopeful and energized and it always works."

I built a magic area I call a magic altar and it works!
Anyone can build one:

Build a magic altar,
a sacred place for dreaming.
Fill it with pictures and symbols,
images that give you meaning.

It's your own creative ritual.
It has magic power.
Write down a wish on paper,
and put it in your altar.

Make sure it's a wish you really want.
Make sure you've thought it through.
Cast a spell in your altar,
you'll find the wish comes true!


What are some creative ways you daydream?

## The Universe Is Listening

I had a spiritually magical experience after a very difficult phone conversation. After the call, I just needed to lie on the bed for a few silent minutes and have a good cry.

As I walked to the bedroom, I passed the living room TV, which was on full volume. I remember thinking, I can't stop to turn it down. I ran in the bedroom, shut the door and plopped on the bed. I could still hear the TV when I started to talk out loud. I told the universe why my experience had been so painful. I cried it out. Then I imagined what the wisdom of the universe would say to me in response and I said that out loud. That made me feel much better so I put my arms around myself as if getting an invisible hug from above. Suddenly I noticed I could no longer hear the TV. No one could have turned it down. I was the only one in the house!

From the doorway, I could see that the TV was on, but there was no sound. I thought to myself, "Oh, I get it. The universe was listening!" And in that second of clarity, the sound popped back on. It was spiritual magic!

Many people in my courses have felt "listened to" or that something or someone was mysteriously communicating with them. Here's what they told the class:

Hal, a freelance computer analyst told us, "I needed money for rent. I had no idea what I was going to do. I said a prayer and tried not to panic. One hour later, my phone rang. I was about to hop in the shower so I didn't want to answer, but something strange was happening. While the phone rang, all the lights on my answering machine lit up at once. That's never happened before. I answered the phone. It was a new client who called to offer me a big project!"

Lola explained, "A good friend of the family had passed on. She loved my mom's cooking. One day my mom was baking bread, and I started to think about our friend. I wish she could come over and feast with us, I thought. At that very moment, a light I thought had been burnt out, suddenly went back on!"

Have you ever felt someone or something was listening to you?

### Make up a poem:

Just as everybody is an artist. Everybody is a poet too, including you!
Writing poems is liberating, creative and exciting. Here's a couple of
poems from some spiritual flirts. My husband and I each wrote a poem. He
wrote the first one, and I wrote the second!

#### Eyes

In the head,
in disguise
there it is,
here it lies
two wise circles,
ready to see
the world out there
and the world of me.

#### Summer Sky

Summer sky
so piercing blue
your clouds are smiling

I'm floating too........

The birds fly
my heart's eye
leaps on the wing

we are soaring........

Make up your own poem right here:

## Take A Magic Walk

Looking for answers? Or maybe an adventure? All you have to do is walk outside. A walk can be one of the most creative and mystical experiences. Walk outside and realize you are on a magic treasure hunt. Clues, signs and treasures will come right to you.

One day I was walking outside daydreaming that I was one of the Beatles. I was imagining I was on stage playing music with them, waving to crowds and entertaining millions. As I daydreamed, I walked by a woman and a little boy, who were out on their front lawn. Right when I passed them the woman said, "Look it's a Beatle!" I froze for a second. Did she hear me daydreaming? Then I turned around and saw that she was pointing to a beetle, the insect kind, on the ground. I giggled to myself enjoying life's magic timing and I went on my way. Just then the little boy shouted, "Bye beetle!" There was magic everywhere!

Here are some comments from other magic walkers:

Steve found some comfort during a difficult time,
"I was having a rough week and started to get really discouraged. I went outside for fresh air. I thought to myself, I need a sign things will get better. Then out of nowhere, a little dog walked up to me. I looked at his dog tag and it said, "Lucky." I felt my luck change at that moment. And it did."

Jennifer said she finds solutions,
"Whenever I walk outside, I feel instant clarity. If I have a problem or if I am confused over something, I just step outside and the answers pop in my head."

Kim had a Disney adventure,
"I went walking outside and passed a tree that had hundreds of birds just chirping away. I stopped to listen for awhile and enjoy their chorus. Then I went on my way, but I noticed the birds kept getting louder. I looked up and the birds seemed to be performing for me. They followed me for a couple of blocks. I realized I'm never alone."

Peter found the perfect advice,
"I was about to give up on a writing project, until I took this walk. Out of nowhere I saw a paper sign that had fallen on the ground. In big black letters it said "Complete." I went home and finished the project."


What have you found on a magic walk?

## Seek Spiritual Role Models

As we create ourselves and flirt with spirituality, we can draw inspiration from people all around us, people who give us strength and nurture our spirit. A spiritual role model can be a family member, a friend or even someone we have never met. It's fun to find ways to connect with our role models and draw energy from their example. My class members shared some of their ways.

Gina's grandmother is her spiritual buddy, "My grandma is so grounded and wise. Just thinking of her makes me centered. I carry a picture of her in my purse. Whenever I feel nervous, I look at it and it calms me immediately."

Pierre said his dog is his role model, "My dog is my hero. He is so loving and so consistent. He saved my life once, and he's been my best friend for five years. His presence makes me feel better immediately, like I have an angel with me."

Dale told us, "My spiritual role model is Muhummud Ali. I have videos of him and a poster in my room. Whenever I need strength, I think of Ali!"


Who are your spiritual role models?


How do you draw energy from them?

## Rhyme or Cheer

At school, we have our cheers. At sport events, we chant. There is special power in rhyming and singing as we use our hearts, minds and voices to bring desired results. As spiritual artists, we can use our chanting power anytime. Here are some cheers, chants and rhymes from other spiritual artists like you and me:

Here's a chant Victor created in class for instant strength:

> "I am calm.
> I am strong.
> I am protected.
> I can't go wrong".

Karen repeated this before her exam,

> "I can get an A,
> my brain will know the way"

Cheryl, a jewelry designer, makes up chants while she works,

> "Jump and swing,"
> you gorgeous new ring.
> You dazzle the hand.
> Just as I planned!"

Make up a chant of your own:

## Make Up Your Own Rituals

When I was young, my mom and I had a little game we used to play.
Whenever we were out shopping and couldn't find a parking place, my
mom would say, "C'mon Jill say your magic prayer." Then I would sing
the words "Pray yay yay yay, yay..." to the tune of "Deck The Halls."
Every time someone would pull out of their parking space at that moment,
and we were in! Rituals are our own creative magic spells.

Here are some rituals from other spiritual artists:

Jeanette told our class, "When I misplace something, and I'm looking for
it, I have this ritual. First I imagine where I left it. Then I point to the spot
I suspect I left it. It's always there."

Allen told us, "Whenever I have a golf tournament, I always wear my
lucky socks. They never let me down."

Frances shared, "Ever since I can remember, I've had this little thing I
recite whenever I travel somewhere. 'I am safe. I am watched. I am well.'
It still makes me feel good."

I love rituals. Whenever I'm in a little bind, I just say out loud "Thank you
Angel," and I always receive help instantly.


What rituals do you have? Make one up.

## Dance or Move

Dancing to music or just simply moving to a beat is creative and freeing. All you have to do is play music that you like. Then feel it, move to it. There are no rules. Like all aspects of flirting with spirituality, it's all about personal expression!

You can:

sway,
jump,
twirl,
tap,
clap,
click,
spin,
jive,
kick,
roll,
rock,

or anything else, in any combination!

What is your favorite kind of music?

Have you danced to it lately?

## Make Cloud Art

One of my favorite things to do is lie down on the grass and watch the clouds pass by. I have a special pair of sunglasses I wear, which really accentuate the clouds texture and bright white color. Clouds contain a wonderfully mysterious and calming energy which is free and available to all us. All we have to do is look up. In my courses, many cloud artists have shared their methods.

Tim, who spends most of the day on the road said,
"Whenever I used to get stuck in traffic I would grow incredibly tense, staring at all the cars ahead and honking my horn. Then I tried looking up. I turn off my radio and watch the clouds. This calms me instantly."

Stephanie said clouds helped her heal,
"Someone I really admired passed away. One particular day my grief was very painful. Then I looked at the sky. Inside one of the clouds, I felt like I saw my friend's face. I could feel her spirit! I felt better instantly. I realized that we are made up like clouds. Cloud energy never dies, it just changes form. Our spirits never die either. We are also energy changing form. I found inner peace right in the sky."

Sally uses imaginary clouds to gain insight,
"When I find myself getting worked up over small things, I imagine myself sitting on a cloud, watching myself from above. I feel safe and protected on the cloud and I can observe myself and my worries from a distant and objective view. It always helps me put things in perspective."


Have you watched a cloud lately?


What are other ways to make cloud art?

Let's review Connect:

*Your spirituality is you're own creative art.
*When we reach out, magic happens.
*Making art out of the world around us brings joy.
*Tune into nature, connect with animals, daydream and imagine.
*Make a poem, create a ritual, move to music, rhyme or chant.
*See the world through a child's eyes.
*Seek spiritual role models, be a spiritual role model.
*Pay attention, the universe is listening.

Everyone is a spiritual artist.

The world is our canvas.

## The Magic Of Flirting With Spirituality

Several years ago, I was watching a program about people in Russia who were living under difficult conditions. I felt for their struggle, and I wondered how can I help? I walked outside, looked up, and said out loud, "If there is any way I can help these people, send my energy over to them." The seed was planted.

Years later, when I wrote my first book, Flirting For Success, my husband and I declared we were starting a flirting revolution, a revolution of warmth, trust, respect, and openness. We would say to each other, "We are the Beatles in Hamburg!" (A city where the Beatles polished their act just before they hit it big.) We imagined our message would spread everywhere and we stayed true to our purpose.

One day as we were talking about the concept for this book, I asked for a sign that we were on the right track. Then we received a letter in the mail from a publisher in Lithuania. They want to translate our first book in Lithuanian! When we eventually received the Lithuanian version, it felt like a definite sign. With it's striking black and red cover and the cry Flirtas!, it has revolution written all over it!

Was my energy sent there? Did my thoughts travel? Had the flirting revolution began? Was our daydream manifesting? Absolutely!

When you flirt with spirituality, you always get magic!

One more quick review......

## M - MEANING
You are the artist of your own destiny.
Follow your heart.

What does your spirit want to do?

## A - AWARENESS
Life gives you magical clues to help you find joy.
Pay attention.

What were some clues you received today?

## G - GRATITUDE
Everything happens for a reason.
Give thanks and feel instant energy.

What are you grateful for in your life right now?

## I - IMAGINE
Thoughts are real.
Imagine the best for yourself and others.

What can you imagine right now to lift your spirits
and change your world?

## C - CONNECT
Magic is everywhere.
Reach out - Life joyfully reaches back.


You are a spiritual artist, what inspires you?




**You are filled with magic, flirt now!**

Do you have a story or experience
involving spiritual magic?

If you want to share your story,
send or fax your letter to me at:

Goal Getters
Attn: Jill Spiegel
3943 Chowen Ave. S
Minneapolis, MN 55410
Fax: 612-922-8241

(Your story may appear in a future book or newsletter!)